DEVOTIONAL
MINUTES
FOR
GIRLS

Jean Fischer

DEVOTIONAL MINUTES FOR GIRLS

INSPIRATION FROM GOD'S WORD

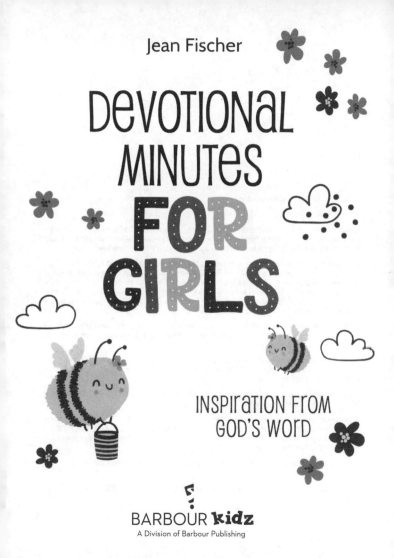

BARBOUR **kidz**
A Division of Barbour Publishing

Print ISBN 978-1-63609-136-5

Published by Barbour Publishing, Inc., 1810 Barbour Drive, Uhrichsville, Ohio 44683, www.barbourbooks.com

Our mission is to inspire the world with the life-changing message of the Bible.

Member of the
Evangelical Christian
Publishers Association

Printed in The United States of America.

001060   0122   SP

INTrODUCTION

There is a special time for everything.
ECCLESIASTES 3:1

One minute. That's all it takes to read each devotional in this book. Each minute will teach you about God, the Bible, and some of the Bible's special and most interesting people. You might even learn a little about. . .*you!* The Bible says there is a time for everything. So set aside one minute each day to spend here with God. Better yet, spend that minute with a parent reading this book together.

• •

Dear God, I can't wait to see what's inside. Let's go! Amen.

SHE HELPED

"This is what the girl from the land of Israel said."

2 KINGS 5:4

The Bible is filled with stories about God and His people. One story tells of a little girl, about your age, who helped a sick man named Naaman. The girl knew about God's friend, a man called Elisha, who made people well. She told Naaman's wife about him. Naaman went to Elisha and was healed. God often uses people to help Him carry out His work. Someday God might use you to help someone too.

• •

Dear God, I would like to be Your helper. Amen.

DADDY'S GIRL

I love You, O Lord, my strength.

PSALM 18:1

God is greater than anything your human brain can understand. He has power over everything. God has always lived, and He will live forever. God made you. He planned everything about you—from what you would look like to who your parents would be. He made you with love, and He will love you forever. God is called "our Father in heaven." You belong to Him, and that makes you a Daddy's girl—someone who is loved bunches and bunches by her heavenly Father.

• •

Dear Father God, I love You too. Amen.

Creator

In the beginning God made from
nothing the heavens and the earth.

GENESIS 1:1

People say, "I love you to the moon and back." That's a big kind of love, isn't it? God made the moon, the sun, and the stars. He made the whole universe in just six days. He created light, sky, land, oceans, plants, trees, animals that live in water, animals that live on land, and birds that fly. God made people too. He loves everything He makes—to the moon and back!

• •

Dear God, I wonder what's beyond
the moon. What can't I see? Amen.

Forever

*God has said, "I will never leave
you or let you be alone."*
HEBREWS 13:5

God knows all about you, even things *you* don't know. He knows what you will do today, tonight, and tomorrow. He knows your future—even who you might marry one day. You can't see yet what God has planned for you. Some things He keeps secret. But you can always trust God to help you. He will never leave you. When He made you, God planned for the two of you to be together forever.

• •

Dear God, thank You for being with me always! Amen.

PEOPLE

"It is not good for man to be alone. I will
make a helper that is right for him."
GENESIS 2:18

People are God's greatest creation. First, He made Adam, a man. So Adam wouldn't be alone, God made a helper for him, a woman named Eve. God made them in His image. That means God wanted them to be like Him and always do what's right. Adam and Eve weren't exactly like God, though. God is absolutely perfect. No one is perfect like Him.

• •

Dear God, help me to be more like You. Amen.

EDEN

The Lord God planted a garden to the east in Eden.
GENESIS 2:8

Adam and Eve lived in a beautiful garden called Eden.
God loaded its trees with delicious fruit. The garden
was like heaven, perfect in every way. There was just
one rule. In the garden, God had planted the Tree of
Learning of Good and Bad (see Genesis 2:17). *"Don't
eat from it,"* God warned. He knew if they ate the
fruit, they would know about not only what was
good but also what was bad—sin.

· ·

Dear God, did they eat from that
tree? I want to know. Amen.

FOOLED!

The woman said, "The snake fooled me, and I ate."
GENESIS 3:13

A sneaky snake came into the garden. It said, "When you eat from the forbidden tree, your eyes will be opened. You will be like God, knowing good and bad" (see Genesis 3:5). *What's wrong with that?* Eve thought. So she and Adam ate the fruit. Then they not only saw the good but also became aware of sin and evil. God was sad they had disobeyed. He made them leave the garden. Their lives weren't beautiful anymore because of sin.

• •

Dear God, don't let me be fooled by sin. Amen.

EVE'S BIG MISTAKE

"Only One can forgive sins and that is God!"
MARK 2:7

Eve gave in to sin. She did what she knew was wrong, and it displeased God. Everyone—even you—is like Eve. We all give in to sin sometimes. We mess up and make mistakes. But when that happens, if we pray and ask God to forgive us, He will. God loves you all the time, even when you do things you know are wrong.

• •

Dear God, I messed up and did something I knew was wrong. I'm sorry. Please forgive me. Amen.

pray

Be full of joy all the time. Never stop praying.
1 THESSALONIANS 5:16–17

Prayer is talking with God. You don't have to talk out loud. If you talk to God in your head, He still hears you. Your heavenly Father loves hearing your prayers. You can tell Him anything, as you would your parents or friends. One of the best things about prayer is you can tell God things you might not be ready to tell others. God hears, and He will help you.

• •

Hi, God. It's me. I've come to talk
with You awhile. . . . Amen.

ALL THE TIME

"Then you will call upon Me and come and pray to Me, and I will listen to you."

JEREMIAH 29:12

God is everywhere all the time. Wherever you are, you can pray and He will hear you. Although there are billions and billions of people in the world, God hears each prayer as if it's the only one. When you talk with God, it's just the two of you talking alone together. Even when everyone around you is busy, God always has time for you.

• •

Dear God, thank You for always being with me. Amen.

MOMS AND DADS PRAY

Hannah was speaking in her heart. Her lips were moving, but her voice was not heard.

1 SAMUEL 1:13

In the Bible we can read the story of Hannah. She prayed for God to give her a baby. She promised God that she would make sure her baby grew up to serve Him. Hannah kept her promise. Her son, Samuel, grew up knowing and loving God. He became a prophet and judge who spoke God's words to the people. When parents pray for their children, God listens.

• •

*Dear God, when my parents pray for me,
You hear their prayers. Thank You! Amen.*

CHILDREN

Children are a gift from the Lord.

PSALM 127:3

God has plans for His children. The Bible includes stories about babies who grew up and did great things. Baby Moses grew up and led the Israelites to a land God promised them. Baby John was born to a woman everyone thought was too old to have kids. As a man, John baptized people and told them about the most special baby of all—Jesus, God's Son. When Jesus grew up, He made a way for everyone in the world to be saved.

• •

Dear God, I wonder. How did Jesus save the world? Amen.

JESUS

Jesus is the Christ, the Son of God.

JOHN 20:31

God sent His Son, Jesus, to earth to help us. First, Jesus was a baby, then a little kid like you. Jesus was different, though, perfect like His Father, God. He grew up to be the greatest Teacher of all. He taught people the right way to live. Jesus is alive and with us today. You can't see Him, but you can believe He is with you and helping you.

• •

Dear Jesus, I can't see You with my eyes, but I can feel You in my heart. Amen.

Forever Life

*"Whoever puts his trust in God's Son will not
be lost but will have life that lasts forever."*

JOHN 3:16

Jesus made a way for people to be rescued from sin.
He was nailed to a cross, and all the world's sins—the
bad things people do—for all time were poured out
on Him. He paid for your sin so you can live with God
forever in heaven someday. Jesus took the punishment
for the bad things people do, so they'd never have to
worry that God wouldn't forgive them if they mess up.

• •

Jesus, Thank You for rescuing people from sin. Amen.

BEST FRIEND

"I am with you always, even to the end of the world."
MATTHEW 28:20

Take a deep breath. You can't see the air you breathe, but it's there. So is God, and so is Jesus. Three days after Jesus died on the cross, He came back to life. He stayed on earth for a little while. Then He went up to heaven to be with God, His Father. Just like God, Jesus is everywhere all the time. He wants to be your friend. Will you pray right now and talk with Him?

• •

Dear Jesus, You are my very best friend. Amen.

GIRLFRIENDS

A friend loves at all times.

PROVERBS 17:17

Can you name three of your girlfriends and tell what you love about each one? Each friend is special in her own way. You are special too. There are tons of things you know how to do that you can share with your friends. There are also things about you that make you a good friend—things like being kind, honest, helpful, respectful, caring, and trustworthy. Think about it. What do your friends love about you?

• •

Dear God, I'm thankful for my friends.
Each is special and loved. Amen.

RUTH AND NAOMI

"I will go where you go."
RUTH 1:16

The Bible tells about two best friends, Naomi and Ruth. Naomi was going to live alone, but Ruth wouldn't let that happen. She promised never to leave Naomi. Ruth was a faithful friend. That means she was a true friend in good times and bad. God is that kind of friend. He promises never to leave you. Are you a faithful friend? Do you stick by your friends in good times and bad?

• •

Dear God, thank You for being a faithful friend. Amen.

SAY HELLO

A man who has friends must be a friend.
PROVERBS 18:24

Making a new friend is as simple as saying, "Hello." The new friends you make will be like you in some ways and different in others. Your differences will help you learn new things about the world and each other. You can never have too many friends. You will find them everywhere—in your neighborhood, at school, at church. . . Can you think of other places?

. . . .

Dear God, I'd like to make some new friends. Please help me find them. Amen.

BE KIND

"Those who show loving-kindness are happy, because they will have loving-kindness shown to them."

MATTHEW 5:7

A good friend is kind. Kindness means doing thoughtful things for others—little things like holding the door open for people, helping when you see someone in need, smiling, saying hello to a new classmate, and doing chores without being asked. Jesus said we should do for others what we would like them to do for us. Can you think of other little ways to show kindness?

• •

Dear God, teach me to be kind
to everyone I meet. Amen.

GOD KNOWS

*"Does He not see my ways
and number all my steps?"*
JOB 31:4

God keeps track of things. He knows how many steps you take and how many hairs are on your head (Matthew 10:30). He knows the number of stars in the sky (Psalm 147:4). When someone cries, God keeps a record of their tears (Psalm 56:8). God sees all you do and every little act of kindness. Try this today: keep track of the kind things you do. How many will you count by bedtime?

. . . .

*Dear God, You know even the
littlest things about me. Amen.*

BE TRUTHFUL

"See, God will not turn away
from a man who is honest."

JOB 8:20

Honesty means telling the truth. God sees everything.
He knows if someone is lying. No one can hide their
actions or even their thoughts from Him. One way
to be a great friend is never to tell lies to or about
anyone. Do you remember that sneaky snake who
got Eve to eat the forbidden fruit? You don't want to
be like him. He was the worst liar of all.

• •

Dear God, please help me
to always tell the truth. Amen.

PERFECT GOD

"God is not a man, that He should lie."
NUMBERS 23:19

God is perfect in every way. God never ever makes a mistake, lies, or does anything wrong. Another name for the Bible is "God's Word," because everything in it is absolutely true. You can always trust God to do exactly what He says. Friends mess up sometimes, but God is the most honest friend you will ever have. You can trust Him with everything all the time.

· ·

Dear God, I know I can always trust You. Everything You say is true. Amen.

Be a Helper

*If someone has the gift of helping
others, then he should help.*

ROMANS 12:7

Friends don't have to be asked to help. They know in
their hearts when someone needs something, and
they jump right in to lend a helping hand. Are you that
kind of friend? If someone needs help, do you see it
right away? It's important to keep your eyes open for
others who are struggling. You could be just the sort
of helper they need.

• •

*Dear God, teach me to know in my
heart when someone needs help. Amen.*

A Special Helper

"The Helper is the Holy Spirit. The Father will send Him in My place. He will teach you everything and help you remember everything I have told you."

JOHN 14:26

The Holy Spirit is your special Helper. He is God's Spirit living inside your heart, the inner voice that teaches you what's right and wrong. The Holy Spirit helps in many ways to keep you strong, safe, and well. He guides you through life and even prays for you in words you cannot hear.

• •

Dear God, thank You for putting Your Holy Spirit inside my heart. Amen.

ResPecT

Show respect for each other.
ROMANS 12:10

The Bible says children should respect their parents, and not just their parents but everyone. Respect means caring that your words and actions don't hurt or upset others. Do you believe your friends think good things when they hear what you say and see how you act? Respect is an important part of friendship. When you respect others, you are also respecting God because He says we should treat everyone with care.

• •

Dear God, I want others to think good things about the way I act and the words I say. Amen.

DISRESPECT

Let no one show little respect
for you because you are young.

1 TIMOTHY 4:12

You know how opposites work. The opposite of up is down, and the opposite of hot is cold. The opposite of respect is disrespect. Disrespect means treating someone badly. You could disrespect someone by saying unkind things to or about them. Being mean to someone or ignoring them is disrespectful too. What would you do if you saw or heard your best friend being disrespected?

. . . .

Dear God, help me to respect others and
to lead them to be respectful too. Amen.

Be a Leader

*Show other Christians how to live by your
life. They should be able to follow you in
the way you talk and in what you do.*

1 TIMOTHY 4:12

Were you ever the leader in a game of Simon Says? You can be a leader every day by setting a good example. Lead others to want to follow the kind things you say and the caring things you do. Try this: use some kind words and actions in a game of Simon Says.

• •

Dear God, please teach me to be a good leader. Amen.

SHare

And do not forget to do good and to share with others, for with such sacrifices God is pleased.

HEBREWS 13:16 NIV

"That's mine!" How would you feel if your friends never shared anything with you? Good friends like to share. They also take good care of things that don't belong to them. Today's Bible verse says that God is pleased when you share. What was the last thing you shared with someone? What was the last thing someone shared with you?

• •

Dear God, I will do my best to please You by being generous with my things. Amen.

Be Generous

The man who gives much will have much, and
he who helps others will be helped himself.
PROVERBS 11:25

A generous friend is a giving friend. Do you remember
our Bible friends, Ruth and Naomi? Ruth gave up her
home and gave her time to make sure her friend Naomi
was cared for and not left alone. Willingly giving up
something you want is called "making a sacrifice." A
sacrifice is the most generous kind of giving.

• •

Dear God, I want to be generous, even when
that means giving up what I want. Amen.

THE GREATEST SACRIFICE

*He sacrificed for their sins once
for all when he offered himself.*

HEBREWS 7:27 NIV

Jesus made the greatest sacrifice of all. He gave up His life so we can live with Him and God in heaven one day. Sin—the bad things people do—isn't allowed in heaven where everything is good and perfect. When Jesus died, He took away all our sin forever. If we ask the Lord to forgive our sins, He will wash our hearts clean and put us in right-standing with Him. Isn't Jesus a generous friend?

• •

Dear Jesus, thank You for Your sacrifice. Amen.

GIrLFrIeNDS HeLPING OTHerS

Each man should give as he has decided in his heart.
2 CORINTHIANS 9:7

Why don't you and your girlfriends get together and come up with some ideas for giving to others? There are so many different ways to give. People sometimes sacrifice money and things, but you could also give someone your time, help, laughter, support, hugs, songs. . . Can you think of other ways to help or make someone happy?

. . . .

Dear God, what are some ways my friends and I can give to others? Will You help us with ideas? Amen.

IT'S ABOUT TIME

There is a time for everything
that happens under heaven.

ECCLESIASTES 3:1

Imagine that everyone is busy and your little sister has no one to play with. There are things you would rather do, but you make time to play with her. Time is a precious gift. Giving others your time is like telling them, "You are important to me—more important than what I want to do." Will you give your time to someone today?

• •

Dear God, teach me to notice
when others need my time. Amen.

BRIGHTEN SOMEONE'S DAY

A faithful helper brings healing.

PROVERBS 13:17

Look around and you will always see someone who needs help. It might be something as simple as holding open a door for someone who is carrying packages. Or it might be a bigger kind of help, like teaching someone to do something or trying your best to comfort someone who is sad. When you give help to someone in need, you brighten their day. Helping will make you feel good too!

Dear God, show me those who need help, and lead me to help them. Amen.

THE GIFT OF JOY

There is a time to cry, and a time to laugh;
a time to have sorrow, and a time to dance.

ECCLESIASTES 3:4

Maybe what someone needs is your gift of joy. Think of how wonderful it would be to turn someone's sad face to a smiley face. What are some ways you can help bring joy to others? It could be encouraging words you speak, something kind you do, even something creative you make. Give others the gift of joy today!

• •

Dear God, please show me someone
who could use a little joy today. Amen.

Careful Laughter

*"How long will those who laugh at
others be happy in their laughing?"*

PROVERBS 1:22

Laughter is another gift you can give. Everyone loves
to laugh at what's funny. But be careful that you lead
others to laugh at the right things. It's never right to
laugh at or make fun of someone. Laughing at something naughty someone says or does isn't right either.
Make sure you help others laugh at the things that
would make God smile too.

* *

*Dear God, may my laughter always
bring a smile to Your face. Amen.*

CARING HUGS

Lord, You have been the place of comfort for all people of all time.

PSALM 90:1

When you get a big hug from your parents or grandparents, it feels good, doesn't it? When someone is sad, a hug can help that person feel cared about and loved. Sometimes God will use you to give a comforting hug to someone who's sad. It's almost like your arms are His wrapped around that person. The gift of a hug is a special thing.

• •

Dear God, please use my hugs to help show Your love and bring comfort to others. Amen.

THE GIFT OF MUSIC

*Is anyone happy? He should
sing songs of thanks to God.*

JAMES 5:13

Music is another gift people can give. Some give concerts to raise money for special causes. Others go to care centers for elderly people and sing songs to those living there. Singing with others brings joy to the world. If you decide to give someone the gift of music, make sure God would approve of the words you sing. Sing as if you are singing to Him.

. . . .

Dear God, I want all of my songs to please You. Amen.

SPECIAL GIFTS

*We all have different gifts that God has given
to us by His loving-favor. We are to use them.*

ROMANS 12:6

Maybe you don't like to sing–that's okay! God gives everyone special things they are good at. Which of your gifts could you share with others? Maybe you're good at teaching younger kids. Maybe you're good at sharing, showing kindness, cheering people up, or working hard to get things done. Use your special gifts to be helpful.

· ·

*Dear God, please show me my special gifts
and ways that I can use them. Amen.*

Recycle

"If you have two coats, give one to him who has none. If you have food, you must share some."
LUKE 3:11

Do you have toys you don't play with or clothes you've outgrown? Recycle them. Give them to someone who can use them. Ask your parents to help you find places in your community where you can donate items to give away. Your toy or that winter coat you've outgrown might be just the gift another kid needs.

• •

Dear God, help me to let go of things I don't need and give them to others. Amen.

Be Caring

"I am here with you as One Who cares for you."
LUKE 22:27

In today's Bible verse, Jesus tells His followers, "I am here with you as One Who cares for you." Jesus is the best caregiver ever. He always cares for you. He also sees when you care for others. Whenever you give your time, help, joy, hugs, songs, or other things you're good at, you are being a caring friend like Jesus. You are serving others—and that pleases God.

· ·

Dear God, I will serve others by
being a caring friend. Amen.

Be Trustworthy

The LORD is trustworthy in all he
promises and faithful in all he does.

PSALM 145:13 NIV

A good friend is trustworthy. That means she keeps her promises and is honest in everything she says and does. She stands up for her friends when others are against them, and they can count on her to be there when they need a little help. A trustworthy friend is always ready to serve others and meet their needs. Jesus is that kind of friend. Are you?

• •

Dear God, I want to be a trustworthy
friend like Jesus. Amen.

GOD'S CHILDREN

God does not see you as a Jew or as a
Greek. . . . He does not see you as a man
or as a woman. You are all one in Christ.
GALATIANS 3:28

God made us to be different, but we are alike in the best possible way—we are His. We are all God's children, and He loves us just as we are. Think about your friends. In what ways are you different? In what ways are you alike?

• •

Dear God, You don't have favorites. We are all
Your children, and You love us the same. Amen.

EVERYONE IS BEAUTIFUL

*I praise you because of the
wonderful way you created me.*
PSALM 139:14 CEV

When God made you, He made you one of a kind.
Everyone is one of a kind; no two people are alike.
God made people to look different from one another—
different skin, eyes, hair. . . Everyone is beautiful in
God's eyes. When God looks at you, He sees you
as His little girl—His precious, beautiful girl. And He
loves you.

• •

*Dear God, thank You for making us one of a kind
and members of Your big, beautiful family. Amen.*

GIRL TALK

Watch your talk! No bad words
should be coming from your mouth.
Say what is good. Your words should
help others grow as Christians.

EPHESIANS 4:29

God hears every word that comes from your mouth. Think about the way you and your friends talk. When you're together, do you use good words? Choosing good words is more than just not saying naughty words or swear words. Good words are kind, caring, and truthful. They can help others feel good about themselves. Good words are always pleasing to God.

. . . .

Dear God, I want my words to please You. Amen.

GOSSIP GIRL

Stay away from gossips–they tell everything.
PROVERBS 20:19 CEV

A "gossip" is a person who tells everything she knows about someone, even when it's secret. Gossips like to talk about other people, and sometimes their talk is hurtful. When one gossip passes her story to another gossip and she tells someone else, the story grows and grows. Too often lies are added to the story, causing even more hurt. Be careful about passing along unkind stories about others. Gossip is never good.

• •

*Dear God, please help me to
stay away from gossip. Amen.*

LIES

A man who tells a lie against his neighbor is like a heavy stick or a sword or a sharp arrow.

PROVERBS 25:18

The Bible says telling a lie about someone is like striking them with a heavy stick or a sword or a sharp arrow. Lies hurt people. Think about how you would feel if a friend told a lie about you. It might make you angry, but you would feel sad too. Friends should always tell the truth to and about each other.

. . . .

Dear God, I will do my best never to lie–about anything! Amen.

52

SNEAKY LIES

*"It is expected of the devil to lie, for
he is a liar and the father of lies."*

JOHN 8:44

Do you remember the sneaky snake in the story of
Adam and Eve? His lie tricked them into eating God's
forbidden fruit. The snake was the devil in disguise.
Some lies sound like the truth, and that's why it's
important to be careful. If you're not sure whether
something is the truth or a lie, ask a grown-up to help
you decide.

• •

*Dear God, please help me know the
difference between truth and lies. Amen.*

HURTFUL TALK

*One who hurts people with bad
talk separates good friends.*
PROVERBS 16:28

Has a person said something cruel or rude to you that
made you cry? Sisters and brothers, and even friends,
sometimes say things they don't mean. When you're
angry, it's wise to think about your words before you
say them. Words can hurt people deep inside their
hearts. If you feel mean words bubbling up inside
you, don't let them out! If you do accidentally say
something hurtful, apologize right away.

• •

*Dear God, may my words be
kind and never hurtful. Amen.*

BE FORGIVING

*"Forgive us our sins as we forgive
those who sin against us."*
MATTHEW 6:12

Jesus said we should forgive those who hurt us. One
of Jesus' followers asked, "If someone asks for forgive-
ness seven times a day, how many times should we
forgive? Seven?" Jesus answered, "Not seven times
but seventy times seven!" (see Matthew 18:21–22).
That's 490 times! Forgiving someone doesn't mean
you should keep letting that person hurt you. Forgiving
a person in your heart pleases God, and it makes you
feel better too.

· ·

*Dear God, please teach me
to be more forgiving. Amen.*

GeNTLe WORDS

A gentle answer turns away anger,
but a sharp word causes anger.

PROVERBS 15:1

Imagine your little brother wants your attention, but you're busy. He keeps at you. You tell him, "Go away! Leave me alone." Sharp words like that cause anger. They can hurt others' feelings too. Gentle words are better. How might you have answered your brother in a gentle way? When you're busy or impatient, it's easy to let sharp words slip out. Try your best to choose gentle words.

• •

Dear God, I will work harder to choose
words that are gentle and kind. Amen.

KIND WORDS

Kind words are like honey.
PROVERBS 16:24 CEV

Kind words are feel-good words. It feels good to say them, and it feels good to hear them. "I like your outfit" is something kind you might say to a friend. There are many kind things you can say to others: "Please." "Would you like to share?" "You're awesome!" "Can I help you?" "Good job!" Can you think of more? Imagine: if you could taste your words, kind words would taste sweet like honey.

• •

Dear God, today I will practice using kind words. Amen.

WISE WORDS

"Follow My teachings and learn from Me."
MATTHEW 11:29

Wise words are some of the best words, because they can teach you amazing things. If you open your ears and listen to wise words, you will learn. Jesus invited people to learn from Him. They listened when He spoke. Jesus used His words to teach the best ways to live right and please God. You can read His words in the Bible in the New Testament books Matthew, Mark, Luke, and John.

• •

Dear God, I want to know what Jesus said. Amen.

SOLOMON

Solomon's wisdom was greater than the wisdom of all the people of the east and all the wisdom of Egypt.

1 KINGS 4:30

The Bible says King Solomon was very wise. He understood many things about life and shared what he knew. If you read the Bible book of Proverbs, you will discover what Solomon had to say. Solomon got his wisdom from God, the best Teacher ever. Listen to God's words, and you'll learn to be wise too.

• •

Dear God, You are the best Teacher. I will listen to and think about Your words. Amen.

WISDOM ALL AROUND

Turn your ear and hear the words of the wise,
and open your mind to what they teach.

PROVERBS 22:17

There's wisdom all around you and much for you to learn. You can get some wisdom by listening to your parents, youth pastors, and teachers. People your grandparents' age and older have tons of wisdom! They've lived a long time and know many things. If you wonder about something, ask. Then open your ears. Listen and learn.

• •

Dear God, thank You for the people in my
life who will help me grow in wisdom. Amen.

DEBORAH

*The Father is the One Who
judges you by what you do.*
1 PETER 1:17

The Bible tells about a wise judge named Deborah. She got her wisdom from God. Deborah held court under a palm tree and judged everyone fairly. She knew what God would say, and she passed His words along to the people. God is the greatest Judge of all. He watches us and judges what we do. Like Deborah's rulings, God's judgments are always fair.

• •

*Dear God, thank You for judging me fairly when
I mess up and do what I know is wrong. Amen.*

FOLLOW THE RULES

God rules over the nations.
God sits on His holy throne.

PSALM 47:8

Did you know God rules over the whole world? He is the King of all kings. God's rules are always fair and good for His people. Along with God's rules are other rules you need to follow. Your parents set rules. So do your teachers. Can you list some of their rules? Following them is important. It shows you are honest, and that pleases God.

• •

Dear God, I know the rules, and I
will do my best to obey them. Amen.

TEN SPECIAL RULES

Honor God and obey His Laws.
This is all that every person must do.
ECCLESIASTES 12:13

Thousands of years ago, God gave a man named Moses ten special rules for everyone to follow. God's Ten Commandments are just as important now as they were then. If you learn the Ten Commandments and follow them, you will get closer to doing what God wants you to do, and that will please Him. Following His Ten Commandments will help you get along better with others too!

• •

Dear God, I want to learn Your ten special rules. Amen.

THE FIRST RULE

"Have no gods other than Me."
EXODUS 20:3

God wanted everyone to know that He is the One and only God. His first commandment says we are to worship no other gods. That means putting God first in our hearts. In the Bible, Jesus says, "You must love the Lord your God with all your heart and with all your soul and with all your mind" (Matthew 22:37). Is that the way you love God? Does He come first in your thoughts every day?

• •

*Dear God, please remind me every day
that in everything, You are first. Amen.*

FaKE GODS

"Do not make for yourselves a god to look like anything that is in heaven above or on the earth below or in the waters under the earth."

EXODUS 20:4

In the Bible, God became angry when His people made a statue of a calf, bowed down to it, and worshipped it. God's second commandment says we are not to worship fake gods. Statues and other objects have no power. They are things created by people. God is the only real God. You should worship nothing but Him. God alone is worthy of your worship.

• •

Dear God, You are the only real God. Amen.

Worship and Praise

"All the earth will worship
You and sing praises to You."

PSALM 66:4

Worship means filling your heart with God's love and loving Him back with your thoughts, your feelings, the ways you act, and the things you do. Praise means telling God and others how great He is and remembering the wonderful things He does. Praise God by telling Him you think He is awesome. Praise Him by singing songs about Him or dancing for Him. You could even draw a picture about something God has done.

• •

Dear God, I will worship and praise You. Amen.

THE THIRD COMMANDMENT

"Do not use the name of the
Lord your God in a false way."
EXODUS 20:7

God's third special rule is about names. God wants everyone to use His name with respect and also Jesus' name and the Holy Spirit's. People are sometimes disrespectful when saying God's or Jesus' names. Doing this is wrong. So is covering up a lie by saying something like, "Honest to God." The names "God" and "Jesus" should always be used in good and respectful ways.

• •

Dear God, help me always to be respectful
when saying Your name. Amen.

A Day of Rest

"Remember the Day of Rest, to keep it holy."
EXODUS 20:8

In six days, God created the sky, the earth, the sea, and every living thing. On the seventh day, God rested. His fourth commandment says we need a day of rest too. Most Christians set aside Sunday as a special day to worship God and rest. Does your family go to church on Sundays? After church, do you take a break from work to relax and have fun?

. . . .

Dear God, I will keep Sunday as a special day to rest and honor You. Amen.

MOMS aND DaDS

"Honor your father and your mother."

EXODUS 20:12

God's fifth rule is about your parents. He wants you to honor your mom and dad. What does that mean? You should respect and obey your parents, not only because you love them but because God gave them to you to help you grow up. Your parents make rules to help you learn the right things to say and do. Could you do better at showing respect to your mom and dad?

• •

*Dear God, please help me to do my best
to respect and honor my parents. Amen.*

THE SIXTH COMMANDMENT

"Do not kill other people."
EXODUS 20:13

Even long ago when God gave Moses the Ten Commandments, people got angry and killed one another. Killing is always wrong. When Jesus said, "'You must love the Lord your God with all your heart and with all your soul and with all your mind.' This is the first and greatest of the Laws," He added, "The second [Law] is like it, 'You must love your neighbor as you love yourself'" (Matthew 22:37–39).

• •

Dear God, I pray that people will stop getting so angry that they kill one another. Amen.

MY PRINCE!

Be faithful in marriage.
EXODUS 20:14 CEV

Do you love stories where a girl and her Prince Charming fall in love and get married? Someday you might get married too. The seventh commandment says you should be faithful to the one you marry. That means putting your partner first before anyone else except God. It means giving him all your love and respect and working together as a team. Remember rule number seven. One day, when you and your Prince Charming marry, you will promise your faithfulness to each other.

• •

*Dear God, have You already chosen
the one I will marry? Amen.*

PLANS

"'For I know the plans I have for you,' says the Lord."
JEREMIAH 29:11

God already knows if you will get married. He already knows who you will marry, if you will have kids, how many kids you will have, and what you will name them! God knows everything. He has your whole life planned. Even before you were born, when He created you, God had a plan for your life. Each day you will discover a little more as His plan for you unfolds.

• •

Dear God, I wonder what You
have planned for me. Amen.

THE EIGHTH COMMANDMENT

"Do not steal."
EXODUS 20:15

How would you feel if someone stole your bike? You would probably be angry and sad too. That bike belonged to you. Stealing—taking something that belongs to someone else—shows that the thief doesn't care about others. It shows he doesn't care about God either. God's eighth commandment says, "Do not steal." Stealing something from someone is like you are stealing from God. It dishonors Him and shows you have no respect for His rules.

• •

*Dear God, I know stealing is
wrong, and I won't do it! Amen.*

I STOLE THaT!

*They must not steal. . .but prove
they can be trusted in every way.*
TITUS 2:10

You might have stolen from others without even noticing. Stealing isn't only about things. If you took someone's place in line, that's stealing. It's also stealing to say someone's ideas or words are your own–like stealing someone's homework. You can steal other people's reputations by gossiping and saying bad things about them. You can also steal a person's trust in you by being dishonest and telling lies.

• •

*Dear God, please remind me that stealing
is more than just taking things. Amen.*

THE NINTH COMMANDMENT

"Do not tell a lie about your neighbor."
EXODUS 20:16

Rule nine says it's wrong to tell lies about others. Some lies can be especially harmful. Jesus' follower John wrote: "Who is a liar? He is a person who says that Jesus is not the Christ" (1 John 2:22). Listen carefully for lies people tell about God and Jesus. When you read the Bible, you will know the truth about who God and Jesus are and the words they say. Everything in the Bible is absolutely true.

. . . .

*Dear God, I will be careful not
to believe lies about You. Amen.*

I WANT THAT

"Do not want anything that belongs to someone else."
EXODUS 20:17 CEV

God's tenth special rule is about jealousy. *Jealous* is a word that means you want what someone else has. Jealousy is when you think things like, *I hate my hair. I wish it looked like hers.* Or, *She gets all the good stuff.* God gives you everything He knows you need. So whenever you feel jealous, thank Him for what you have. Your gratitude will please Him. It will help you feel better too.

• •

Dear God, I'm grateful for what I have. Amen.

A Memory Game

"Keep these words of mine in
your heart and in your soul."
DEUTERONOMY 11:18

Are you good at remembering things? How many of the Ten Commandments can you say without looking them up? You will find them in the Bible in Deuteronomy 5:7–21 and Exodus 20:3–17. It's good to memorize Bible verses. When you store them inside your heart, you will have them ready to help whenever you need them. Try to memorize one verse each day.

. . . .

Dear God, I will memorize Your words
and keep them in my heart. Amen.

sLeepover

I will lie down and sleep in peace.
O Lord, You alone keep me safe.

PSALM 4:8

Sleepovers are fun! There might be music, games, food, movies. . .but when it's time to sleep in an unfamiliar place, you might feel a little uneasy. There's a Bible verse to memorize for that: "I will lie down and sleep in peace. O Lord, You alone keep me safe." Whether you're at home or away, you'll sleep peacefully knowing God is with you.

• •

Dear God, I will fall asleep thinking of
You, knowing You are with me. Amen.

NIGHT

He knows the number of the stars.
He gives names to all of them.
PSALM 147:4

You can see God's greatness all around you in the nighttime. Fireflies come out and blink their greetings to each other. You can hear God's owls calling, *"Whooo. . .whooo. . ."* Animals like raccoons and armadillos wander around looking for things to eat. Look up, and you'll see a sky filled with stars. God made each one. He knows how many there are. He's even given them names.

• •

Dear God, day and night I see Your
greatness all around me. Amen.

CLOUDS

"He covers the face of the moon and spreads His cloud over it."

JOB 26:9

Do you enjoy seeing clouds form different shapes? Maybe you'll see a cloudy rooster float by, or a dolphin, a car, a feather, a heart. . . Clouds are harder to see at night. But when the moon is full and bright, clouds sometimes float by and cover part of its face. Look up at the moon. If you see a cloud race by, say today's Bible verse.

• •

Dear God, I love watching animal-shaped clouds and clouds racing past the moon. Amen.

BEAUTIFUL YOU

The sun has one kind of glory while the moon and the stars have another kind. And the stars differ from each other in their beauty and brightness.

1 CORINTHIANS 15:41 TLB

Everything has its own kind of beauty—the sun, the moon, the stars, and people! Every person is beautiful in their own way. *You* are beautiful. It's not just how pretty you are on the outside. You are beautiful because of what's inside your heart. The best thing about your loveliness is that your sunny personality lights up the world.

• •

Dear God, You made me beautiful inside and out. Amen.

A Beautiful Heart

*Your beauty should come from the
inside. It should come from the heart.*
1 PETER 3:4

When you invite Jesus to live in your heart, His love grows inside you. If you listen to what Jesus says is right and if you do what is right, your heart will become even more beautiful. A heart filled with Jesus' love helps you to use gentle words and show respect for others. A beautiful heart is a strong heart ready to do every good thing.

• •

Dear Jesus, thank You for my beautiful heart. Amen.

A CLean HearT

Your Word have I hid in my heart,
that I may not sin against You.

PSALM 119:11

Your heart is where you store God's Word—the wise things you learn from the Bible. When you memorize a Bible verse, it will be there in your heart, ready when you need it. The Bible has good advice to help you live in ways that please God. When you live to please Him, then your heart will be pure and clean, just the way God wants it.

• •

Dear God, I want to live to please You. Amen.

masterpiece

We are the clay, and You are our pot maker.
All of us are the work of Your hand.

ISAIAH 64:8

A "masterpiece" is a precious work of art, one of a kind and lovely in its own special way. You are God's masterpiece! When He makes people, God creates them just the way He wants them. Each one is beautiful and perfect in His sight. Take a look in the mirror and thank God for making you just the way you are.

• •

Dear God, I like the way You made me. Amen.

NOTICE ME!

*Christian women should not be dressed in the kind
of clothes. . .that will make people look at them.*
1 TIMOTHY 2:9

Which do you think is more important: how you act
or what you wear? Looking clean and neat is important. But some people dress for attention. They want
others to like them because they wear expensive
clothes. Your true friends will like you no matter what
you wear, and they will love you because you're you.

• •

*Dear God, I am beautiful not because of what I
wear but because of what's in my heart. Amen.*

keep it clean

A beautiful woman who does not think
well is like a gold ring in the nose of a pig.

PROVERBS 11:22

Imagine a freshly washed pink piggy with a lovely gold ring in her nose. Everyone says, "Look how pretty she is!" But then that piggy jumps in the mud and gets all dirty and stinky. Today's Bible verse reminds us not to allow our beautiful, clean hearts to get dirty by thinking and doing things that don't please God.

• •

Dear God, I will keep my heart clean by pleasing
You with my thoughts, words, and actions. Amen.

LYDIA

*One of the women who listened sold
purple cloth. . . . Her name was Lydia
and she was a worshiper of God.*

ACTS 16:14

What's your favorite color to wear? The Bible tells about Lydia, who sold purple cloth. Do you think she wore purple clothes? Lydia knew God, but she didn't know Jesus. One day, Jesus' follower Paul saw Lydia sitting near a river. Paul sat down and shared the Good News about Jesus saving us from sin. Lydia asked Jesus to come into her heart and stay there forever.

• •

Dear God, I'm glad Lydia learned about Jesus. Amen.

GOOD NEWS

*"The feet of those who bring
the Good News are beautiful."*

ROMANS 10:15

The Bible books Matthew, Mark, Luke, and John are called "the Good News." They tell Jesus' story from the day He was born. Jesus wants His story told to everyone. In Bible times, people got around by walking. Some walked for miles and miles just to share the story of Jesus' life. Maybe that's why the Bible says, "The feet of those who bring the Good News are beautiful."

• •

*Dear Jesus, Yours is the greatest story
ever told, and every word is true. Amen.*

88

FOLLOW JESUS

"Go and make followers of all the nations."
MATTHEW 28:19

Jesus chose twelve special helpers. These men were His "disciples"—followers who learned from Jesus and shared what they learned. They were the first of many Jesus followers. You can be a Jesus follower too. As you learn about Jesus, tell others what you know about Him. Share the Good News that Jesus died to save people from their sin. He made a way for us to get to heaven.

• •

*Jesus, I will learn the story of Your
life and share it with others. Amen.*

LOVe LiKe JeSUS

"I give you a new Law. You are to love each other.
You must love each other as I have loved you."

JOHN 13:34

Jesus said the most important of God's laws is to love God with all your heart. The next most important is to love others the way Jesus loves them. Jesus' kind of love means loving people even if you're angry or upset with them. Jesus' love is a patient and forgiving kind of love.

. . . .

Dear Jesus, I want to learn to love others the
way You love them. Please help me. Amen.

Love Is. . .

*Those who do not love do not
know God because God is love.*

1 JOHN 4:8

Jesus' follower Paul wrote about love. He said love is patient and kind. It's not jealous. Love is being humble. Love does what's right. It's unselfish. It doesn't get angry. It forgives. Love hates what's bad and loves what's true. Love doesn't give up. It believes in and hopes for the best. Love keeps on going. It never ends. The Bible says God is love. He loves with a love that is perfect.

. . . .

Dear God, love has so many parts! Amen.

Be Patient

A person's wisdom yields patience.
PROVERBS 19:11 NIV

How do you act when you want to go someplace but your parents aren't ready? Do you whine and complain, or are you patient? Patience isn't always easy. It takes practice, and it's something you learn. Each time you try your best to be patient, you are learning the kind of patience God wants you to have. He is patient with you all the time. Remember that, and when it's hard to wait, ask God to help you.

• •

Dear God, please help me to be patient. Amen.

WHAT IF?

Do not let yourselves get tired of doing good. If we do not give up, we will get what is coming to us at the right time.

GALATIANS 6:9

God wants you to be kind to others. But what if they aren't kind in return? Today's Bible verse has the answer. God sees when you are kind, and He has a plan to reward your kindness. Don't expect a reward right away, though. Keep doing what is good, and God will bless you with His goodness.

• •

Dear God, I will keep being kind and doing what is good. Amen.

BLESSINGS

Our LORD and our God, you give these
blessings to all who worship you.
PSALM 144:15 CEV

God gives you His blessings. That means God gives
you good things. His blessings are everywhere—a
loving family, good health, happy times shared with
friends. . . Can you think of more ways God blesses
you? God wants you to bless others. That means He
wants you to do good things for them. You are helping God to bless others when you treat them with
kindness and love.

. . . .

Dear God, thank You for Your many blessings. Amen.

JOSEPH'S STORY

*Wherever you find jealousy and
fighting, there will be trouble.*

JAMES 3:16

In the Bible story about Joseph, we read that his brothers were jealous because they thought their dad liked Joseph best. His brothers were so jealous that they tricked Joseph and sold him as a slave. Jealousy leads to trouble. Jealous feelings keep you from loving others. If you have jealous feelings inside your heart, ask God to help you turn them around. How did Joseph treat his jealous brothers? He forgave them and treated them with love.

. . . .

*Dear God, please help me get
rid of my jealous feelings. Amen.*

Pretty Princess

*The person who thinks he is important
will find out how little he is worth.*

MATTHEW 23:12

Imagine a princess who shouted from her balcony,
"Look at me! Don't you think I'm lovely?" Those who
heard the princess decided she was stuck up, and they
looked the other way. Jesus said to be humble—that
means *not* telling the world how great you are. Paul
wrote that love is always humble. You show love by
not bragging about yourself but instead helping others
to feel good about themselves.

• •

Dear God, will You remind me to be humble? Amen.

Be an Encourager

*Therefore encourage one another
and build each other up.*
1 THESSALONIANS 5:11 NIV

Imagine you are talking with your best friend. Finish this sentence: "You are so good at _____." We love others by encouraging them—helping them to feel good about themselves. You can encourage with words: "I know you can do it!" "Good job!" "I love what you did." But encouragement is more than just words. It's celebrating with others the things they accomplish and showing others you love them just as they are.

• •

Dear God, I want to be an encourager. Amen.

RIGHT AND WRONG

*But even if you suffer for doing
what is right, you will be happy.*
1 PETER 3:14

Name something that's wrong to do. Next, name something you know is right. You understand the difference. Some friends might want you to do what's wrong. But don't. What happens if you get caught doing what's wrong? You get punished, and that's no fun. God sees when you do the right thing, and He says you will be happy if you do what's right.

• •

*Dear God, please guide me
to choose what's right. Amen.*

KEEP DOING WHAT'S RIGHT

*Do not be afraid or troubled by what
they may do to make it hard for you.*

1 PETER 3:14

Jesus' disciples did their best to set a good example.
Even when people made it hard for them, they didn't
give up. They kept doing what was right. You can set
a good example too. Show your friends how a Jesus
follower talks and acts. Even if they make it hard for you,
you'll be showing them love by teaching what's right.

• •

*Dear God, help me to set a good
example for others. Amen.*

SELFISH LITTLE PRINCESS

An unfriendly person pursues selfish ends and
against all sound judgment starts quarrels.

PROVERBS 18:1 NIV

Imagine a princess who never shares her things. If anyone asks to share, she shouts, "No! That's mine!" If someone touches her things, she says, "Leave it alone. It's mine!" That little princess doesn't have many friends. Her selfishness starts quarrels. Sharing with others would be a loving thing for her to do, because it would show that she cares about others.

. . . .

Dear God, I don't want to be like a selfish
little princess. I would rather share. Amen.

THE GRUMPY, GROWLY KING

Don't make friends with anyone
who has a bad temper.
PROVERBS 22:24 CEV

Imagine a kingdom ruled by a grumpy, growly king. He's always so angry that his subjects don't want to be around him. The Bible tells us to have nothing to do with a person like that. A good king is like God. He rules with love. If a good king is angry at all, it's because he wants people to do what's good and right. God, the Great King, wants only what's best for His people.

• •

Dear God, You rule the world with love. Amen.

BOOM! Fireworks!

Get over your anger before the day is finished.
EPHESIANS 4:26

Everyone gets angry sometimes. Anger can catch us by surprise. It bubbles and builds up inside us and then–*boom!*–it explodes like fireworks. Anger causes us to say and do things we otherwise might not. Can you think of a time when your anger hurt someone you love? Today's Bible verse reminds you not to hold on to your angry feelings. Let them go before the day is done.

. . . .

*Dear God, please forgive me for those times
when my anger has hurt someone. Amen.*

LOVE MEANS FORGIVING

Then Jesus said, "Father, forgive them.
They do not know what they are doing."
LUKE 23:34

Some people were angry with Jesus for no good reason. They hated Him because He said He was God's Son. They nailed Jesus to a cross and left Him there to die. As He was dying, Jesus said to His Father, God, "Father, forgive them. They do not know what they are doing." Jesus loved those who hated Him. He forgave them even when their anger was wrong.

. . . .

Dear God, help me to be forgiving like Jesus. Amen.

HaTe WHaT'S BaD

*The whole Bible. . .is useful to teach us what is true
and to make us realize what is wrong in our lives;
it straightens us out and helps us do what is right.*

2 TIMOTHY 3:16 TLB

When Paul wrote about love, he said love means
hating what's bad. When you turn away from sin—the
bad things you want to do—you show God that you
love Him. You show Him that instead of choosing sin,
you choose to follow His rules from the Bible. And
your obedience pleases Him.

. . . .

*Dear God, I will show You I love
You by doing what's right. Amen.*

LOVE WHAT'S TRUE

Love is not happy with sin.
Love is happy with the truth.

1 CORINTHIANS 13:6

The Bible teaches you right from wrong. When you do what the Bible says is right, God sees. He loves to see you working at being patient and kind. He celebrates when you aren't jealous or acting stuck up. He is delighted when you calm your anger and truly forgive those who have hurt you. Love is the happy feeling that comes from pleasing God by doing what's right and true.

• •

Dear God, doing what's right makes me happy. Amen.

weary LIttLe Princess

Love takes everything that comes without giving up.

1 CORINTHIANS 13:7

Imagine a little princess who grew weary of being patient, kind, and forgiving. "Loving others is hard work!" she said. Her words were true. Love can be hard work sometimes. But the harder you work at loving others when you're young, the easier it is to love as you get older. Today's Bible verse says love doesn't give up. The little princess decided not to give up on love. It was a very wise decision.

• •

Dear God, I will keep on loving
even when it's hard. Amen.

Believe!

Love believes all things. Love hopes for all things.
1 CORINTHIANS 13:7

When loving is hard, the Bible says we should keep believing in the goodness of others. If someone acts in an unloving way, talk with God about it. Ask Him to help you love that person. If someone you know is always doing what's wrong, ask God to help that person do what's right. Love always hopes for things to get better and believes that God will help.

• •

*Dear God, I believe in Your goodness–
and that gives me hope. Amen.*

GOD'S PERFECT LOVE

Give thanks to the LORD, for he
is good. His love endures forever.
PSALM 136:1 NIV

King David wrote many of the Bible's psalms—songs
that worship God. One of his songs, Psalm 136, is
about God's everlasting love. God's love is perfect.
God's love is great. Best of all, God's love is forever.
God loved you when He made you. God will love you
all through your life. And when you get to heaven
someday, you will meet God and understand just
how much He loves you.

• •

Thank You, God, for Your goodness and love. Amen.

GROWING AND CHANGING

"For I, the Lord, do not change."

MALACHI 3:6

Look at how grown up you are! Every day you are growing and changing. Everything around you is changing too. The seasons change. So does the weather. Shadows change. Can you think of other things that change? People and the world are always changing, but **God does not change. His love for you won't change.** You can always trust Him to be your best friend and the same wonderful, loving God—no matter what!

• •

*Dear God, I know I can always
trust You. Thank You! Amen.*

WANTS AND NEEDS

God can give you all you need.
He will give you more than enough.

2 CORINTHIANS 9:8

What do you need today? A need is something necessary, like food, water, and a place to live. God knows what you need, and He will give it to you. But God often gives you more than you need. He gives you what you want. Think about all the things you have that you don't really need. Those are gifts from Him.

. . . .

Dear God, thank You for providing what I
need and also giving me things I want. Amen.

ADVENTUrOUS YOU!

O taste and see that the Lord is good.
How happy is the man who trusts in Him!

PSALM 34:8

The world is a big, wonderful place with much to explore. Every day is like an adventure. Do you enjoy trying new things? Be adventurous! Taste a food you haven't eaten before. Try out a new hobby or sport. Make new friends. God is good, and He has placed many good things in His world for you to discover.

* *

Dear God, open my eyes to new and exciting
things to discover and explore. Amen.

GOD, GIVE ME STRENGTH!

I can do all things because
Christ gives me the strength.

PHILIPPIANS 4:13

Maybe you feel a little afraid to get out into the world and do some exploring. The world might seem too big and unfamiliar. Don't let those butterflies in your tummy stop you from having adventures. Pray and ask God to give you strength to stand up to fear. Face those butterflies and say, "Butterflies, butterflies, go away, because I'm going to try something new today!"

• •

Dear God, when I feel afraid,
I will put my trust in You. Amen.

David and Goliath: Part 1

You are my safe place in the day of trouble.
JEREMIAH 17:17

Standing up to fear is like David standing up to Goliath. The story is in the Bible: God's army, the Israelites, fought an evil group of soldiers, the Philistines. One of the Philistine soldiers, Goliath, was big, strong, and almost twice as tall as most men. When the Israelite soldiers saw him, they ran away from him, afraid. But a brave young shepherd boy named David wasn't afraid to fight Goliath. David knew God was on his side.

• •

Dear God, You keep me safe. Amen.

David and Goliath: Part 2

"You come to me with a sword and spears.
But I come to you in the name of the Lord."

1 SAMUEL 17:45

David picked up five stones and his sling—a weapon for shooting stones. He ran toward Goliath. The giant laughed and made fun of him. David put one stone in his sling and fired. It hit Goliath on the forehead. Down he fell! David didn't need a sword or spear. God gave him everything he needed to fight his enemy.

. . . .

Dear God, You help me to be brave. Amen.

TALENTS

These gifts help His people work well for Him.

EPHESIANS 4:12

When you try new things, you'll discover that you're better at some than others. Maybe singing or acting will come easily to you. Or you might find you're great at making something or teaching or taking care of animals. God gives all of us special gifts called "talents"—things we're good at. When you discover your talents, keep working at them. Ask God to show you how to use them to serve Him.

• •

Dear God, thank You for helping me discover what I'm good at. Amen.

SErVING GOD

"If anyone wants to be My follower, he must
forget about himself. He must. . .follow Me."

MATTHEW 16:24

Serving God means obeying Him and doing what He
wants. Sometimes God will ask you to be brave and
do something that might make you feel uncomfort-
able. To be God's follower, you have to forget about
yourself and about feeling afraid and instead trust
that God knows what He's doing. When He asks you
to do something and you follow through, then you
are being God's servant and doing His work.

• •

Dear God, I will be Your servant. Amen.

Moses

"I know that You can do all things.
Nothing can put a stop to Your plans."

JOB 42:2

God had great plans for Moses. But Moses was afraid. He didn't speak well. He didn't want to stand up to important men and say the words God wanted him to say. But nothing stops God's plans. God gave Moses a helper to speak his words. God also gave Moses courage. Moses became a great leader—one of the greatest in the Bible.

• •

Dear God, when I think I can't do something,
give me helpers and the courage to try. Amen.

CONFIDENCE

So do not throw away your confidence;
it will be richly rewarded.
HEBREWS 10:35 NIV

Confidence is a big word that means "being sure of yourself." When you've practiced your part in the play and you're sure you know all your lines, that's confidence! When you learn what God says in the Bible, you can be sure what you've learned is true because the Bible doesn't lie. Then when you put into practice what you learn, you will have confidence knowing what you're doing is right.

• •

Dear God, help me to have confidence
I'm doing what's right. Amen.

PLEASING GOD

Christian brothers, we ask you, because of the Lord Jesus, to keep on living in a way that will please God.
1 THESSALONIANS 4:1

Knowing what's right is easy because the Bible clearly describes the kinds of thoughts, words, and actions that please God. Jesus' follower Paul wrote that good behaviors (things like love, joy, peace, patience, kindness, goodness, gentleness, faithfulness, and self-control) are like delicious fruit growing on a healthy tree. When you practice good behaviors, you can have confidence you are pleasing God.

. . . .

Dear God, I want my behavior to please You. Amen.

LOVE IN ACTION

You obey the whole Law when you do this one thing, "Love your neighbor as you love yourself."

GALATIANS 5:14

You've learned what the Bible says about love. Now let's put some of that love into action. Who are your neighbors? Your neighbors are everyone! When Jesus said, "Love your neighbors," He meant everyone in the world should love each other. Can you think of a way you could send some love to a child who lives on the other side of the world?

• •

Dear God, my love can stretch all the way across the world. Amen.

JOY TO THE WORLD!

"I will have joy in doing good to them."
JEREMIAH 32:41

Jesus' follower Paul sent his friend Tychicus to visit a church far away. In a letter to the church, Paul wrote that Tychicus could "bring joy to your hearts" (Colossians 4:7–8). What do you think it means to bring joy to someone's heart? Spreading joy around is fun because joy is "contagious"—it's catching. Can you think of one way you can bring joy to a loved one's heart? Can you think of one way to send joy to someone across the world?

• •

Dear God, sharing joy with others is fun! Amen.

peace

God blesses those people who make peace. They will be called his children!

MATTHEW 5:9 CEV

You are God's child, and you have an important job. That job is to bring peace into the world. If all God's children get together and work at being at peace with each other, the world will become a better place. Peace starts with you. It means getting along with others and also helping others to get along. What could you do today to bring about peace?

• •

Dear God, please guide me to help make the world a more peaceful, pleasant place. Amen.

KEEP GOING

"Tell the people of Israel to keep going."
EXODUS 14:15

The Israelites got tired of walking to the great new land God had promised them. God said, "Keep going." If they had given up, they would have missed out on all the good things God had planned for them. When things get hard, you need to keep going too. God has a plan for you. Do you wonder how big and wonderful it is? If you give up, you will never find out.

• •

Dear God, maybe Your plan for me will change the world. Amen.

Pay It Forward

You must be kind to each other.
EPHESIANS 4:32

What does it mean to "pay it forward"? When you do something kind for someone, you can encourage that person to do something kind for someone else. If you give your friend a cookie and she says, "Thank you," you could say, "Pay it forward." Paying it forward is a great way to spread kindness all over the place! So don't forget: when someone does something kind for you, pay it forward.

· ·

*Dear God, please remind me to repay
every kindness shown to me. Amen.*

124

GOODNESS!

"My people will be filled with My goodness," says the Lord.

JEREMIAH 31:14

God's goodness is all around you. He shows His goodness by giving you what you need and, sometimes, what you want. He gives you people who love and care for you. God's goodness is seen in things like a warm, sunny day and a puppy's wet kisses. It is everything that makes you happy! God loves when you tell others about His goodness. Who needs to hear about God's goodness today?

• •

Dear God, thank You for being so good to me. Amen.

FAITHFULNESS

Jesus said to them, "Have faith in God."
MARK 11:22

God is pleased when you share love, joy, peace, kindness, and goodness. But something else pleases Him even more—your faithfulness. It means obeying and trusting Him, no matter what. God is faithful to you. He is with you in good times and in bad. Even when He's not pleased with your behavior, God loves you. Practice being faithful to Him. God is the best friend you will ever have.

• •

Dear God, You never leave me or let me down. I will love and trust You always. Amen.

GENTLENESS

Be gentle and kind. Do not be hard on others. Let love keep you from doing that.

EPHESIANS 4:2

When you treat others with gentleness, God is pleased. Imagine your little sister picking up a black crayon and scribbling all over your pretty drawing. She's too young to know what she did is wrong. You could be angry with her, or you could be gentle and explain why it's not nice to draw on someone's picture. People remember when you treat them gently, and God will too.

. . . .

Dear God, help me to treat others with gentleness. Amen.

SELF-CONTROL

Like a city whose walls are broken through
is a person who lacks self-control.
PROVERBS 25:28 NIV

Little Princess was angry because the queen wouldn't let her go to the ball. "You're not the boss of me!" she shouted. She shouted so loudly that the castle walls came tumbling down! The Bible says a person who lacks self-control is like a city whose walls are broken through. Self-control means calming down your bad feelings. It's being the boss of your feelings and doing what's right.

• •

Dear God, I will be the boss of my
feelings and do what is right. Amen.

THANKFULNESS

*Go into His gates giving thanks and
into His holy place with praise. Give
thanks to Him. Honor His name.*

PSALM 100:4

You have so many good reasons to thank God. He
loves you. He brings you joy and peace. He helps you
keep going when you want to give up. He is kind to
you, good and gentle. God is always faithful. He will
always forgive you when you do what is wrong. He
will never leave you. Can you think of other reasons
to thank Him?

• •

Dear God, thank You so much for everything! Amen.

SHHH. . .QUIET

Be quiet and know that I am God.
PSALM 46:10

God is pleased when you spend quiet time alone with Him. You can spend that time praying and talking with Him. You can spend quiet time reading and thinking about Him. You could just be alone someplace lovely and appreciate that God made that place and put you there. Spend quiet time with God every day. It is the best way to know Him even better.

• •

Dear God, let's get together. I love spending quiet time with You. Amen.

Quiet Prayers

Never stop praying.
1 THESSALONIANS 5:17

Jesus is God. He hears your prayers even when you *think* them. You don't need to pray out loud. You can pray to Him quietly. Jesus is interested in everything you do. You can ask Him for help or just spend time with Him when you feel lonely. You can talk as much as you want about anything at all! He loves hearing your voice. Talk with Jesus using your own words, just as you would with a parent or friend.

• •

Dear Jesus, let's talk. I have things to tell You. Amen.

SON OF GOD

*We are joined together with the true God
through His Son, Jesus Christ. He is the
true God and the life that lasts forever.*

1 JOHN 5:20

Jesus is God's Son. Just like God, Jesus has lived forever
and He will never die. When God sent Jesus to earth
as a human, He had a purpose—to make us ready for
heaven one day. Jesus is the One who connects us with
God, our heavenly Father. We can live in heaven with
God someday because we believe in Jesus.

• •

Dear Jesus, I love You. Amen.

A Special Baby

Jesus said to them, "Yes, have you not read the writings, 'Even little children and babies will honor Him'?"

MATTHEW 21:16

Jesus came into the world the way you did, as a baby. God had great plans for Him. Jesus would grow up to save people from their sin. When Jesus grew into a man, even little children knew how special He was. They honored Jesus with praise, calling out to Him, "Greatest One! Son of David!" (Matthew 21:15).

• •

Dear Jesus, when You were born, did people know how special You were? Amen.

A SIMPLE BEGINNING

She put cloth around Him and laid
Him in a place where cattle are fed.

LUKE 2:7

Where were you born? In a hospital? At home? The Bible says Jesus was born in a place where cows were fed. He didn't have a cozy bed or doctors and nurses caring for Him. God planned for Jesus to have a very simple beginning. But this baby who was born in the simplest possible way would grow up to do the greatest thing of all.

• •

Dear God, You make even simple things great. Amen.

A SPECIAL NIGHT

*"I bring you good news of great
joy which is for all people."*

LUKE 2:10

It was an ordinary night, but God was about to do something extraordinary. Shepherds were watching their sheep when an angel appeared in a bright, heavenly light. He told them Jesus had been born. "There will be something special for you to see. . . . You will find the Baby with cloth around Him, lying in a place where cattle are fed" (Luke 2:12). Then the sky filled with angels praising God.

• •

*Dear God, I wish I could have seen the
angels on the night of Jesus' birth! Amen.*

DO YOU BELIEVE?

*When they saw the Child, they told
what the angel said about Him.*

LUKE 2:17

The angel told the shepherds that this baby, Jesus, was the One who would save the world from the punishment of sin. The shepherds went to see Him. They told everyone what the angel had said. All who heard it were surprised. Do you think they believed the shepherds' words? Jesus' mom, Mary, believed. She hid those words in her heart and thought about them much.

• •

*Dear Jesus, I believe! God sent You to save
us from the punishment of sin. Amen.*

THE STAR

"We have seen His star in the East.
We have come to worship Him."

MATTHEW 2:2

God set a bright star in the East. Wise men who studied the stars saw it. They believed if they followed the star, they would find Jesus. They knew He was special. They believed that someday He would be a great leader of the Jewish people. But they didn't yet know how great Jesus would become. They followed the star and brought Jesus gifts fit for a king.

• •

Dear Jesus, You would grow up to be
greater than a king—any king! Amen.

KING OF KINGS

He is the King of kings and Lord of lords.
1 TIMOTHY 6:15

Jesus grew up in a town called Nazareth, but then He moved on. He traveled around teaching people about God, showing them the right way to live. Everywhere He went, people followed wanting to hear Him speak. They knew Jesus was special, but they didn't know yet He was the Son of God. One day they would understand—Jesus is the King of all kings, the Lord of all lords, the world's Savior.

• •

Dear Jesus, I'm glad I know who You are. Amen.

FAITH

*"He speaks to the wind and the
waves and they obey Him."*

LUKE 8:25

One night, Jesus and His disciples were in a boat on a lake in a big storm. While Jesus slept, huge waves rocked the boat from side to side. "Wake up! We're going to die!" the disciples shouted. Jesus got up. "Be still!" He told the storm. The wind and waves stopped. "Where is your faith?" Jesus asked His friends. Wherever you go, Jesus is with you. Have faith that He will help you.

• •

Dear Jesus, You will always help me. Amen.

WALKING ON WATER

"Is anything too hard for the Lord?"
GENESIS 18:14

One evening Jesus wanted to be alone to pray. He told His disciples to take the boat to the other side of the lake. "Go on ahead of Me," He said. They were in the boat in the dark of night when they saw someone walking on the water toward them. "It's a spirit!" they cried. But it was Jesus. Can you imagine a man walking on water? An ordinary man, apart from Jesus' power, couldn't. But Jesus can do *anything*.

• •

Dear Jesus, there is nothing You can't do. Amen.

DOUBT

"Why did you doubt?"
MATTHEW 14:31

Jesus' follower Peter said, "'If it is You, Lord, tell me to come to You on the water.' Jesus said, 'Come'!" (Matthew 14:28–29). Peter climbed out of the boat and walked on the water toward Jesus. But when he thought about what he was doing, Peter started to sink. Jesus lifted him out of the water with His strong hands. When you doubt that you can do something, remember this story. Keep trying. When you think you can't, Jesus will be there to lift you up.

• •

Dear Jesus, I will trust You always. Amen.

OPPOSITES

*"He that is faithful with little things
is faithful with big things also."*
LUKE 16:10

Faith and doubt are opposites. Faith means believing in something. Doubt means not believing. Put your faith in Jesus, and He can help you do anything in His plan for you. If you trust Him, Jesus will help you do little things—for example, strapping on a harness and helmet and scaling a climbing wall. When you get better at little things, Jesus will help you do bigger things. Maybe one day you'll climb a mountain!

• •

Dear Jesus, I have faith in You. Amen.

Bread and Fish

"It is true! This is the One Who speaks for
God Who is to come into the world."

JOHN 6:14

A crowd of five thousand people gathered to hear
Jesus speak. The people were hungry. There was no
food to feed them. But then Jesus took a young boy's
lunch of bread and fish and made it grow and grow
until there was enough for the whole crowd. It was a
miracle! People began to understand that Jesus came
to them from God.

· ·

Dear Jesus, no one else could make
a small lunch grow so big! Amen.

miracles

"Where does he get all this wisdom and the power to work these miracles?"

MATTHEW 13:54 CEV

A miracle is something wonderful that happens that can't be explained. Jesus made miracles happen when He lived here on earth. He made sick people well. He made blind people able to see again. He healed people who couldn't walk so they could run! Jesus even brought people back to life from being dead. These amazing things happened because of Jesus. He has all of God's wisdom and power.

. . . .

*Dear Jesus, You are powerful and wise.
Thank You for working miracles! Amen.*

COMPANY'S COMING!

Everyone in his house put their trust in Jesus.
JOHN 4:53

When Jesus traveled, He often stayed as a guest in someone's home. Many people learned about the right way to live when Jesus stayed with them. They understood how special He was and put their trust in Him. Some even became Jesus' close friends. Can you imagine Jesus as a guest in your house? How would you treat Him if He came to visit? Would you want to be His friend?

• •

Dear Jesus, You are always welcome
to come to my house. Amen.

MARY AND MARTHA

*Mary sat at the feet of Jesus
and listened to all He said.*

LUKE 10:39

One time Jesus visited His friends, sisters named Mary and Martha. Martha was busy making dinner for Jesus, while Mary sat listening to Him talk. Martha became upset. "Jesus," she said, "tell her to help me!" Gently, Jesus told Martha that listening to what He had to say was more important than preparing a nice meal. Listening to Jesus and learning from Him are more important than anything!

• •

*Dear Jesus, I will stop what I'm
doing and listen to You. Amen.*

BIBLE STORIES

*Everything that was written in the Holy
Writings long ago was written to teach us.*
ROMANS 15:4

The Bible includes many true stories like Mary and
Martha's. With each story you read, you will learn
something important about God and living to please
Him. You can read about great moms who raised
their kids to serve God. There's the story of Miriam, a
big sister who saved her baby brother, and the story
of Queen Esther, who rescued her people from an
evil plan.

• •

*Dear God, I love reading about Bible people
and learning from their stories. Amen.*

Eve's Story

The man called his wife's name Eve,
because she was the mother of all living.

GENESIS 3:20

Who was the first mom ever? Eve! She's the one who ate the forbidden fruit in God's garden. Eve didn't have a mom. God put her in the garden just like He did Adam. But later, Adam and Eve had kids. Eve became the first mom to teach her children to obey God. Ever since, moms have been teaching their children to love God and respect Him.

• •

Dear God, thank You for moms who
teach their kids to love You. Amen.

JOCHEBED'S STORY

*She took a basket made from grass, and
covered it with tar and put the child in it.*

EXODUS 2:3

Moses' mom, Jochebed, was brave. An evil ruler wanted
all the baby boys killed. But Jochebed wasn't going to
let that happen to her baby. She made a little basket
for Moses, and she hid him in the tall grass at the edge
of a river. Then she told Moses' big sister, Miriam, to
stay and watch over him, making sure he was safe.

• •

*Dear God, thank You for helping
Jochebed keep her baby safe. Amen.*

149

MIRIAM'S STORY

His sister stayed to watch and find
out what would happen to him.

EXODUS 2:4

The evil ruler's daughter, a kind princess, found Moses. She felt sorry for the baby and decided to keep him. Miriam had an idea. "I know of a nurse who would help care for the baby," she said. Then Miriam brought Jochebed to the princess, keeping secret the fact that Jochebed was Moses' mom. "Raise the child until he can eat on his own," the princess told Jochebed. And so Jochebed took her baby home!

• •

Dear God, thank You for saving Moses' life. Amen.

THE PRINCESS'S STORY

The child grew, and [Jochebed]
brought him to Pharaoh's daughter.
EXODUS 2:10

Baby Moses was saved! Jochebed cared for him until he could eat on his own. Then came the sad day when she had to give Moses back to the princess. The princess raised him as her own son. God had saved Moses from dying, because He had a great plan. Moses would grow up to be one of the greatest leaders of all time, a true man of God.

• •

Dear God, You had a plan for Moses.
You have a plan for everyone. Amen.

MaN OF GOD

Moses the man of God prayed. . .that good
would come to the people of Israel.

DEUTERONOMY 33:1

A man or woman of God is someone who is happy to obey God and live by His rules, even when life is hard. Can you think of grown-ups you know, either men or women, who love and obey God? If you start trusting God and living right, you will become a woman of God— strong, brave, and willing, like Jochebed and Miriam.

• •

Dear God, someday I will be
called a woman of God. Amen.

PRINCE CHARMING

Who can find a good wife? For she
is worth far more than rubies.

PROVERBS 31:10

Do you ever pretend you're grown up and married?
One day you might find your real Prince Charming. The
Bible says a good wife is more precious than rubies—
beautiful, sparkling red jewels. Of course, in God's
eyes, you're already more precious than rubies just
the way you are. But one day, in addition to becoming
a mighty woman of God, you might become someone's precious wife.

• •

Dear God, do You already have my real
Prince Charming picked out for me? Amen.

Faithful Princess

The heart of her husband trusts in her, and
he will never stop getting good things.

PROVERBS 31:11

If Prince Charming made you his princess, he would know he could trust you with everything. You would be faithful to him. That means you would keep your promises. Prince Charming would be sure he could count on you to keep the castle running smoothly. Practice being faithful to God, and He will prepare you to be a trustworthy wife to a real Prince Charming in the future.

• •

Dear God, teach me to be faithful to You. Amen.

Goodness, Gracious Princess!

*She does him good and not
bad all the days of her life.*

PROVERBS 31:12

One of your princess jobs would be bringing good-ness into the castle. What does that mean? It means being gracious—doing your best to act like Jesus would by being kind, caring, gentle, patient, and loving. Goodness is setting an example for others of obey-ing God's rules and living to please Him. When you practice goodness now, you are getting yourself ready to be a good wife and mom someday.

. . . .

Dear God, please help me to practice goodness. Amen.

LITTLE PRINCESS WORKS-SO-HARD

She. . .works with willing hands.

PROVERBS 31:13

How willing are you to do your chores? If someone asks you to pick up your toys or help set the table, are you willing to do it? Do you offer to help without being asked? A faithful princess is willing to work hard. She knows things have to get done, and she does them without grumbling. Are you a grumbler, or do you work willingly to get the job done?

• •

Dear God, I'm sorry for being a grumbler sometimes.
Please help me to work willingly. Amen.

156

Princess in the Kitchen

She brings her food from far away.

PROVERBS 31:14

Do you like to bake cookies? Maybe you've helped to make sandwiches, salads, spaghetti, or mac and cheese. When you help in the kitchen and learn to cook, you are preparing yourself to make good, healthy meals for your own family someday. God created all kinds of fruit, veggies, and other good things that you can put together to make meals. Would you make an elegant dinner for you and Prince Charming to share?

• •

Dear God, thank You for good food to eat. Amen.

GET UP, PRETTY PRINCESS!

*She rises while it is still night and makes
food for all those in her house.*

PROVERBS 31:15

Do your parents need to tell you over and over every morning to get up? God has all kinds of good things waiting for you today, but you'll miss some if you spend your time lying in bed. One day when you're married to Prince Charming, it will be your job to get up early, make breakfast, and tell your children, "Get up!"

• •

*Dear God, help me to wake up each
morning, ready for the day. Amen.*

A Royal Project

She makes herself ready with strength,
and makes her arms strong.

PROVERBS 31:17

Imagine your Prince Charming is planning a special building project—maybe a royal treehouse for your royal children. He needs your help. Would you be ready with strong arms and plenty of energy? Taking care of your body now by eating right and getting exercise will help make you ready. God gave you your body. It's up to you to work at keeping it healthy and strong.

• •

Dear God, I will take care of my body
by exercising and eating right. Amen.

Princess with a Lamp

Her lamp does not go out at night.

PROVERBS 31:18

On sad days when everything feels dark, God's love is like a softly glowing lamp that brings comfort. His kind of light is a reminder that He's with you and everything will be okay. You could be the kind of princess who lights up the world for your family and others. If your royal husband or royal children felt sad, would you show them some love to help them feel better?

• •

Dear God, please teach me how to
light up the world with love. Amen.

160

A GIVING PrINCESS

She opens her hand to the poor, and
holds out her hands to those in need.

PROVERBS 31:20

Do you care about sharing what you have and helping others? Of course you do! You're a princess in training. You're preparing for that day when you and your Prince Charming will be caring and giving toward everyone in the kingdom. You'll be an honorable and generous couple, ready and willing to help anyone in need. And your giving hearts will please God.

• •

Dear God, I want to please You by
being generous in my giving. Amen.

ROYAL ROBES AND GOWNS

Her clothes are strength and honor.
PROVERBS 31:25

A royal princess should look elegant but not over-done. There's such a thing as too much! Wild clothing, too much makeup, and too much perfume have no place in a majestic castle. Starting now, practice dressing in a way that's neat, clean, and brings honor to the kingdom. Then, when you're all grown up, your real Prince Charming will say, "Don't you look lovely today!"

. . . .

Dear God, I will honor You by caring for myself but not putting too much focus on my appearance. Amen.

LiTTLE PrinCeSS POSiTiVe

She is full of joy about the future.
PROVERBS 31:25

Positive and negative are opposites. A positive outlook means you see the bright side of things. A negative outlook means you see things in a dark, dreary way. Good and bad attitudes can be catching. A good attitude is like spreading sunbeams all over the castle. A bad attitude is like spreading germs. Be a positive princess. Shout to the kingdom, "Today is a great day! Tomorrow will be even better!"

• •

Dear God, help me to see the
bright side of things. Amen.

SOFT-SPOKEN PRINCESS

*She opens her mouth with wisdom. The
teaching of kindness is on her tongue.*
PROVERBS 31:26

A wise princess is careful about what she says. Her
words set a good example for everyone in the kingdom. Her words are soft-spoken–said in a gentle, quiet
voice. If Prince Charming tells his princess something
in secret, she won't tell others. That would be gossip.
A princess's words should always be kind. She should
teach others to speak in ways that please God.

. . . .

*Dear God, please help me to
choose my words wisely. Amen.*

BUSY, BUSY PRINCESS

*She looks well to the ways of those in her house,
and does not eat the bread of doing nothing.*
PROVERBS 31:27

No! You won't command ladies-in-waiting to do all
your work for you. You're the kind of princess who's
always working. If you see something that needs to
be done, you get right in there and start. There's no
time to be lazy. God gave you an important job—
to keep the castle looking great and running smoothly.
You enjoy being a busy, busy princess!

• •

*Dear God, when I feel lazy, please lead
me toward something to do. Amen.*

Praiseworthy Princess

Her children rise up and honor her. Her husband does also, and he praises her.
PROVERBS 31:28

You are an amazing and hardworking princess. You do an awesome job managing the inner workings of the castle. You treat everyone in the kingdom with kindness. Your Prince Charming and royal children stand up and say, "We love you, Princess Mom! Good job!" Praising others—telling them they've done well and thanking them—is important. Have you thanked your mother today?

• •

Dear God, my mom is amazing! I will honor her and thank her for all she does. Amen.

SHE HONOrS GOD

*A woman who honors the
LORD deserves to be praised.*
PROVERBS 31:30 CEV

When the princess receives praise for her good works, she gives her praise to God. He's the One who helps her get through each day. When she's tired, God gives her strength. When Prince Charming and the children are crabby, God helps the princess to be patient and forgiving. The princess prays all through her day and thanks God for the many ways He helps her.

• •

*Dear God, I honor and praise You
for all the ways You help me. Amen.*

QUEEN ESTHER

*"And now, O Lord God, You are
God. Your Words are truth."*
2 SAMUEL 7:28

It's fun to pretend. But remember—when you read about princesses and kings and queens in the Bible, those people were real. Their stories are true. The Bible tells of a real queen named Esther. She was a beautiful Jewish girl from a poor family who married powerful King Ahasuerus. He ruled 127 parts of his nation, from India to Ethiopia. But there was trouble in his kingdom. . . .

• •

Dear God, I want to know more of Esther's story. Amen.

COUSIN MORDECAI

And every day Mordecai walked in front of the open space of the house. . .to learn how Esther was.

ESTHER 2:11

Esther's parents died when she was young. Her older cousin, Mordecai, was like a dad and cared for Esther. When Esther became queen, Mordecai still showed concern for her well-being. Every day, he walked outside the castle wanting to know if Esther was okay. That's what parents do. They care about their children even when they're all grown up, like Queen Esther.

• •

Dear God, thank You for my parents
who love and care for me. Amen.

AN EVIL PLAN

But their plan became known to
Mordecai and he told Queen Esther.
ESTHER 2:22

Mordecai overheard the king's servants plotting to kill the king. Mordecai told Esther, and she told King Ahasuerus. Esther saved her husband's life! But one of the king's trusted men, Haman, was angry with Mordecai. He tricked the king into agreeing with a plan to kill Mordecai and all the Jews. What would Esther do? Could she get the king to save her people?

• •

Dear God, I think You had a plan to save
the Jewish people. Am I right? Amen.

THE RIGHT TIME

"Who knows if you have not become queen for such a time as this?"

ESTHER 4:14

Mordecai told Esther she needed to stop King Ahasuerus from carrying out Haman's plan. Bravely, Esther went to her husband. "O king," she said, "I ask that the lives of my people be saved" (see Esther 7:3). Esther was able to get the king to see that his trusted servant, Haman, was tricky and evil. It was the right time for Esther to be queen. She saved the lives of her people, the Jews.

. . . .

Dear God, You did have a plan. You always do. Amen.

A Time for Everything

*Everything on earth has its
own time and its own season.*
ECCLESIASTES 3:1 CEV

God had Esther exactly where she needed to be at the right time. God has you where you need to be too. He put you on earth when He wanted you here. He has a special purpose for your life. You probably won't marry a prince or a king, but God will lead you to help make the world a better place—when the time is just right.

. . . .

Dear God, when the time is right, I'll be ready. Amen.

FOLLOW GOD'S PLAN

*Let us keep running in the race
that God has planned for us.*

HEBREWS 12:1

God's plans are perfect in every way. Sometimes people choose not to obey God and mess up His plans. Jonah was one of those people. God wanted Jonah to go to a certain city to preach, but Jonah ran away. He ended up spending time in the belly of a big fish! His story is a reminder to go where God leads you. He knows what He's doing.

• •

*Dear God, Your plans are always perfect.
Help me to follow them. Amen.*

JONAH

*"Can a man hide himself in secret places
so that I cannot see him?" says the Lord.*
JEREMIAH 23:24

Jonah tried to hide from God. He hurried away on a ship, and he was thrown overboard. A big fish swallowed Jonah. He was in its belly for three days! God saw what happened. He was with Jonah the whole time. When Jonah asked God for help, the big fish spit Jonah out on dry land. Jonah had learned that wherever you go, you can't hide from God.

• •

God, I will do my best never to hide from You. Amen.

Perfect Plans

The plans of the Lord stand forever.

PSALM 33:11

If you were to disrupt God's plan by disobeying Him, running away, or trying to hide, God would still find a way to make His plan work. God's plans are perfect. Nothing gets in their way. Even before you messed up His plan, God would know. He would already have a backup plan waiting. You can trust forever that God will do exactly what He plans. Why? Because He's the One and only all-powerful God.

· ·

*God, I'm grateful I can always
trust in Your plans. Amen.*

ANGELS

For God did not give us a spirit of fear. He gave us a spirit of power and of love and of a good mind.
2 TIMOTHY 1:7

Jonah was afraid inside the belly of the fish. But God was there with him. When you are afraid, God is with you too. He will even send angels to protect you. Remember this Bible verse: "For He will tell His angels to care for you and keep you in all your ways" (Psalm 91:11). Thinking about God's army of angels will help you be brave.

• •

Dear God, thank You for angels! Amen.

176

WORDS TO REMEMBER

[The Bible] gives the man who belongs to God
everything he needs to work well for Him.

2 TIMOTHY 3:17

It's important to remember Bible verses because they can calm you when you face trouble. Bible verses help when you're scared, tired, sick, worried, lonely, or sad. There are Bible verses for everything! Memorize God's Word so you will have it in your heart whenever you need it. Can you say any Bible verses from memory? Try to memorize a new verse every day.

• •

Dear God, please help me to memorize Your
words and keep them in my heart. Amen.

ANGELS ALL AROUND

"Do you not think that I can pray to My Father? At once He would send Me more than 70,000 angels."
MATTHEW 26:53

Before Jesus died, He said that if He asked, God would send more than 70,000 angels to protect Him. But Jesus didn't ask for angels. He knew God had a greater plan. Although you can't see them, God's angels are all around you. And just like Jesus, you can ask God to send them to help you whenever you need them.

• •

Dear God, whenever I need help,
please send me Your angels. Amen.

ANGELS IN DISGUISE

Do not forget to be kind to strangers and let them stay in your home. Some people have had angels in their homes without knowing it.

HEBREWS 13:2

The Bible suggests you could meet a stranger sometime who is really an angel in disguise. What does that mean? It means you should be kind to everyone you meet and do your best to treat them in ways that please God. You'll never know if you might have shown kindness to an angel God sent your way.

• •

Dear God, I wonder—have I met an angel? Amen.

FUN TO BE YOUNG

But the LORD said to me, "Do not say, 'I am too young.' You must go to everyone I send you to and say whatever I command you."

JEREMIAH 1:7 NIV

You're a little girl. This is your time to enjoy being young. Play dress-up. Pretend. Have fun with your friends. But don't ever think you are too young to learn something new. Each day you will move a little closer to becoming a grown-up. Take your time, though. God will get you there soon enough.

• •

Dear God, I love being a kid. Amen.

GAMES KIDS PLAY

Anyone who runs in a race must follow the rules to get the crown.

2 TIMOTHY 2:5

Do you have a favorite game? There are many fun board games, and sport games too, like basketball and soccer. You and your friends might enjoy playing tag or Simon Says, card games or dominoes. Whatever **games you play, following the rules is important.** Anything else is cheating, and that's not pleasing to God or to those you are playing with.

• •

Dear God, whatever games I decide to play, I will follow the rules. Amen.

Dancing Shoes

Let them praise His name with dancing.

PSALM 149:3

Do you like to dance? The Bible says when a man named Jephthah came home, his daughter met him with music and dancing (Judges 11:34). Have you danced for your daddy? Put on your tutu and dance a ballet for him, or dance to your favorite song. Have you ever danced for your heavenly Father? Dancing is one way to worship God. Dance respectfully to honor Him. Create a dance to celebrate God's greatness or to show your love for Him.

• •

Dear God, I will worship You with dancing. Amen.

Take Turns

*Value others above yourselves, not
looking to your own interests but each
of you to the interests of the others.*

PHILIPPIANS 2:3–4 NIV

Whatever fun things you do with your friends, remember to take turns. Maybe you want to play a board game but your friend wants to play with dolls. Let her have her way sometimes. When you take turns doing something each of you enjoys, you will get along better. Taking turns is another way of sharing and showing you care.

· ·

*Dear God, please remind me to
take turns when I play. Amen.*

CHILD OF GOD

*For the Holy Spirit speaks to us and tells
our spirit that we are children of God.*

ROMANS 8:16

There will be days when you and your friends don't get along and days when you feel like nobody understands you. On those days, it's important to remember who you are. You are a child of God! When you're feeling down, listen to that voice in your heart that says, "You are God's kid." Cheer up! God is right there with you, and better days are coming.

. . . .

Dear God, I'm grateful because I am Yours. Amen.

HAPPY BEING YOU

I am not trying to please people.
I want to please God.
GALATIANS 1:10 CEV

Even when you are doing your best to be kind and caring toward others, there will be times when someone is displeased with something you do. You won't please everyone all the time. Don't let that make you sad. Be happy being you! You know who you are—God's girl. Always do your best to behave in ways that please Him, and you will be okay.

. . . .

Dear God, when You are pleased
with me, I am happy. Amen.

More to Learn

*But Jesus said, "Let the little children
come to Me. Do not stop them."*
MATTHEW 19:14

You've learned a lot about God, but there's so much
more to learn. Read your Bible and ask questions. Look
for answers. Memorize Bible verses so you will have
them ready when you need them. Remember that
God will forgive you whenever you mess up. He loves
you. Jesus does too. God welcomes you. Talk with Him
all the time. Ask Him to lead you today and every day.

. . . .

Here I am, God. What will You teach me today? Amen.

Treasures

This is the day that the Lord has made.

PSALM 118:24

Each day is like a treasure hunt. It holds something new to add to your treasure chest. You might discover a new friendship or a new hobby—something you're really good at, something you'll love. Maybe something will happen today that you'll want to remember forever. That memory will go into your treasure chest too. This is the day the Lord has made! Today and every day, thank Him for all that you treasure.

· ·

Thank You, God, for every day and
every little treasure. Amen.

Scripture Index

OLD TESTAMENT

NEW TESTAMENT